32 Chichewa
Phrases and Conversations
By Karen Roller

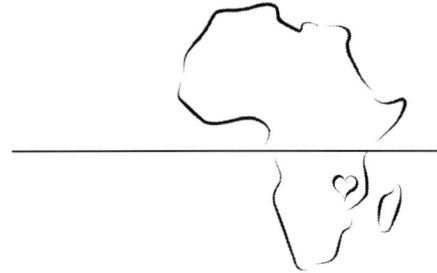

32 Chichewa Phrases and Conversations

© March 2017 by Karen Roller

Illustrations by Katy Chong

All Rights Reserved

ISBN-13: 978-1544722566

ISBN-10: 1544722567

Photo Credits:
Front Cover: Karen Roller
Page 6: Kelsie Graber
Page 28: Paul and Stephanie Byrne
Page 78: Carmen Hortenberry

Dedicated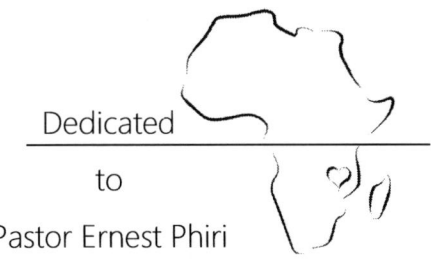
to
Pastor Ernest Phiri

You taught me to love Malawi,

to love your people and to speak your language.

Thank you, dear friend.

With love,

        Karen Roller

With love, Karen

I am so glad you're heading to Malawi, my favorite place on earth! I love her mountains, her lake, her weather, but mostly her people.

As a small child, I dreamed of having an orphanage some day where I would care for a hundred children. Every time our family would move, I would find a house in the area I thought might be big enough for my hundred children. In Malawi, I found the children I had planned for all those years and a place that finally felt like home.

For the past 10 years, I've taken many people to Malawi to meet my beautiful children, my amazing Malawian friends and to see what God is doing among us at the Grace Center in Dowa District, Malawi.

Cross cultural friendships are challenging and absolutely amazing! I pray as you prepare for your trip and as you land in Malawi that God will give you the grace of language to communicate with your new friends. May you build friendships that will endure far beyond a one-time trip and may you visit Malawi again and again in the years to come!

Special thanks goes to my daughter, Katy Chong, for her beautiful illustrations. I'm sure glad we let you draw murals all over your rooms as a child! Thank you for reliving a little of your Africa life through these pages.

I also want to express gratitude to my friend, Melissa Ingram, for encouraging me and making endless lists and edits to help me finish this project.

My husband, Leonard, is a gem unlike any other. He supports me, encourages me, picks me up and never lets me down! This book would not be here without his dedication and love.

With love,

Karen Roller

Introduction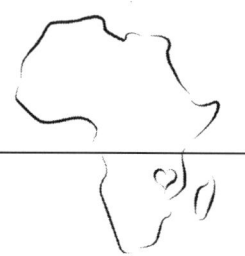

Communication is the key to being able to share our stories and learn from each other. This is often one of the biggest challenges short-term team members face when traveling to another country. This book is designed to help you communicate and build relationships in Malawi.

The book has three sections: 20 Words or Phrases, 12 Conversations, and a Glossary.

The first section gives you cultural insight into 20 words or phrases commonly used in Malawi. Each lesson has a pronunciation guide, the English translation, a practice exercise to help you become familiar with the phrase and a cultural segment called Go Deeper.

The second section has 12 conversation guides. These guides have English/Chichewa questions and answers along with pictures and clues to lead you through a conversation with a child or adult. There are extra pages included in this section where you can draw your own pictures or have someone else draw a picture to help you understand each other better.

The Glossary section has a list of common English words and their Chichewa translation along with a few sample sentences of how to use the word in Chichewa.

A general guide to pronunciation:

In Chichewa the vowels are very short and simple as opposed to our English vowels, which draw out sliding diphthongs.

A = AH as in awe

E = long A as in cake

I = long E as in seat

O = long O as in coat

U = OO as in loose

Table of Contents

Section One: 20 Words and Phrases..p 6

    1. Thank you!........................p 10

    2. How are you?...................p 11

    3. I am fine..........................p 12

    4. See you later....................p 13

    5. Sleep well........................p 14

    6. I love you!.......................p 15

    7. I'm happy to see you!......p 16

    8. I'm sorry..........................p 17

    9. Mother/Father..................p 18

    10. Pastor............................p 19

    11. Child/Children................p 20

    12. Let's go!.........................p 21

    13. Laugh!...........................p 22

    14. What is your name?........p 23

    15. I am from......................p 24

    16. How old are you?...........p 25

    17. Let's pray!......................p 26

    18. I will miss you!..............p 27

    19. You did it!.....................p 28

    20. Stay well!......................p 29

Section Two: 12 Conversations..p 31

    1. The Pointing Game..p 32

    2. Body Parts...p 36

    3. Animals Around the Village..p 40

    4. Wild Animals..p 44

    5. Things Around the Village..p 48

    6. Playing Games..p 52

    7. Things at School...p 56

    8. Talking about School..p 60

    9. Do you speak Chichewa?..p 64

    10. My Family..p 68

    11. All About Work..p 72

    12. Talking About Jesus...p 76

Section Three: Glossary...p 81

Section One

20
Words and Phrases

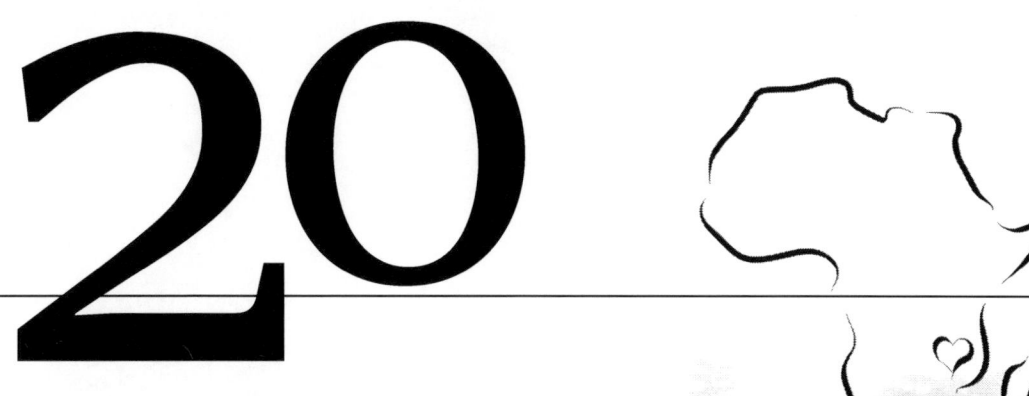

Zikomo

Zee-kō-mō

Thank you

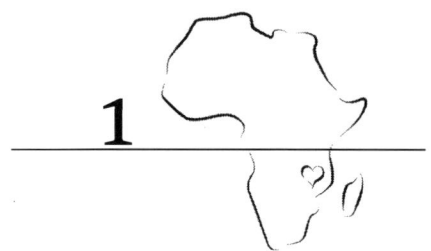

Practice

Say *Zikomo* to everyone you meet today. You can hold the door for someone and say, "*Zikomo*! It means thank you in Chichewa!" You can pick up your cup of coffee and say, "*Zikomo* for my coffee. That means thank you in Chichewa." It will be great practice for you and a cool opener for talking about your up-coming trip to Malawi.

Go Deeper

If you only learn one word before you go to Malawi, learn this one: *Zikomo*.

This very useful word means thank you! It can also be used for "Excuse me," "You're welcome," and "I don't have a clue what I'm doing, but I'm trying to speak your language!"

The word *zikomo* can get you out of a lot of situations. A vendor walks up to you and wants to sell you his mouse kabobs; shaking your head vigorously, you run away, saying, "*Zikomo*!"

Perhaps you are walking through a village and everyone is greeting you with rapid phrases you cannot understand. You politely clap your hands together without making a sound and say, "*Zikomo, zikomo*!" Suddenly, you move from stranger to friend.

The first step to breaking down the barriers of cross-cultural communication is to take a sledge hammer to your fear and embarrassment about speaking another language. It really doesn't matter if you make mistakes. You just need to go for it. Your new friends will appreciate your effort.

Muli bwanji?

Moo-lee bwah-njee

How are you?

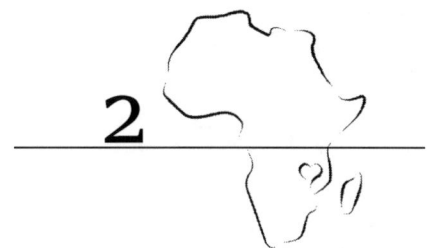

Practice

Make it your goal today to ask 20 people how they are. Just make sure you ask them in Chichewa! You can say, *"Muli bwanji?* How are you?" Don't worry at this point if you don't know the answer in Chichewa. Just be bold and ask, *"Muli bwanji? Muli bwanji?"* 20 times!

Go Deeper

Greetings are extremely important in African cultures. Before any other conversation takes place, be sure to greet everyone in the room. At this point, you only have our first two phrases: *Zikomo! Muli bwanji?* But you've covered some of the most important relationship ground.

Chichewa has greetings for morning, afternoon, and evening, as well as greetings for leaving and arriving back home. Often greetings will include asking about the household, the children and extended family members. During the rainy season, greetings almost always include an inquiry regarding fields and crops.

One of my biggest mistakes as a expat is to skip the greetings. Westerners often get caught up in the necessity of what they have to say and will barge into a room beginning the conversation without even a simple hello. A proper greeting sets the stage for a great conversation. In Africa, pause, take a breath, and greet everyone; build the relationship from the very opening of conversation.

Ndili bwino, kaya inu?

Ndee-lee bwee-nō, kī-yah ee-noo

I am fine, what about you?

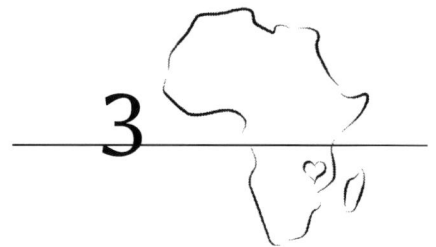

Practice

Today, you're going to put our first three phrases together to make a full greeting. The greeting exchange goes like this:

Muli bwanji?
　　　　Ndili bwino, kaya inu?
Ndili bwino.
　　　　Zikomo!

Go Deeper

Ready to dig a little into some other greetings?

Kudzuka: to wake up

Mwadzuka bwanji? How did you wake up this morning?
　　　　Ndadzuka bwino, kaya inu? I woke up great, how about you?
Ndadzuka bwino. I woke up great!
Zikomo! Zikomo!

Kuswera: to go through the day
Mwaswera bwanji? How's your day going?
　　　　Ndaswera bwino, kaya inu? It's going great, what about you?
Ndaswera bwino! It's going great.

Zikomo! Zikomo!

You get the idea! Try putting *Kuyenda* into that same sequence. How did you travel?

Mwayenda bwanji? Ndayenda bwino! Zikomo! Zikomo!

Tionana

Tee-oh-nah-nah

See you later!

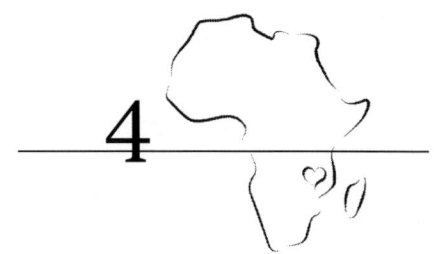

Practice

Instead of saying bye today, say *Tionana*! See you later! You can say it on the phone, your email, or in person! Try to keep the tee at the beginning very short, don't let your long e sound drag out too long. When your English speaking ears hear Malawians say the tee sound, you may almost hear it too-oh-nah-nah. Chichewa vowels are very quick. Practice saying *tionana* without allowing any extra diphthongs to sneak in.

Go Deeper

The verb *Kuona* means to see. If we add the ending -na to the verb, we get a reciprocal effect. The beginning prefix ti- is the conjugation for the third person plural, we.

Literally, *tionana* means we'll see each other. The tense is a future perfect tense. So the ti-syllable needs to be pitched slightly higher than the other syllables.

Here is a little bit of fun for you:

-Lankhula means to talk. *Tilankhulana* means we'll talk together soon.

You try this one: *-vetsera* meaning to understand. Can you encourage someone that you're working on learning Chichewa and you'll understand each other soon? Check at the bottom of the page!*

Relationships are extremely important in African cultures. When we don't have the ability to communicate with language, we must find other ways to express our desire for relationship. While you're working on the language, a handshake, sitting with someone even if you can't talk, and the effort to keep meeting together goes a long way to bridging the gap.

*Tivetserana

Gonani bwino.

Gō-nah-nee bwee-nō

Sleep well.

Practice

You will recognize the word *bwino* from our second lesson. It means good or well. Be sure to wish everyone a good night of sleep as you go to bed tonight! *Gonani bwino!*

Go Deeper

The verb *kugona* means to sleep. It is used here in a polite command form. When you say to someone "*Gonani bwino,*" you are encouraging him or her to have a good night of sleep. You can also say "*Usiku wabwino,*" which literally means good night.

The verb *kugona* can also mean to lie down. You can tell someone who needs to lie on the exam table in the clinic "*Gonani.*" Or tell a child who isn't feeling well "*Gonani*" to rest on the porch of the school for a few minutes. *Tulo* is the noun for sleep.

Malawi is located just 13° south of the equator. When the sun sets at 6 pm, the darkness of night falls swiftly. As Westerners, we are more accustomed to a lingering twilight with plenty of warning that night is coming soon.

Roughly less than 10% of the population of Malawi has access to electricity, which makes the night even darker. One bonus that comes with less light pollution is an absolutely amazing view of the stars. The Milky Way shimmers with brilliance. The Malawi starry night will give you a whole new appreciation for the Psalmist's words, "The heavens proclaim the glory of God. The skies display his craftsmanship...night after night they make him known. They speak without a sound or word; their voice is never heard. Yet their message has gone throughout the earth, and their words to all the world." Psalm 19:1-4 NLT

Ndimakukondani

Ndee-mah-koo-kō-ndah-nee

I love you!

Practice

This is a fun one and easy to practice. Just tell all your loved ones today, "*Ndimakukondani*, I love you in Chichewa!" If you can't find 20 people you love, you may have to tell some of them more than once or make a few new friends.

Go Deeper

One of my favorite Malawian couples is a very unlikely pair! She is tall and quite large for a Malawian, and he is short and very skinny, no matter how well he eats! She is rough and hard. He is gentle and full of laughter; when he talks about his wife, his eyes flood with tears of joy as he shares how much he loves her. Yes, Malawians fall in love!

The tradition of marriage (whether by love or arrangement), paying the bride price, and fulfilling all village and family requirements is still alive and well in Malawi. The months of August – October are the wedding months! At the time of marriage, rather than bridesmaids or groomsmen, the couple each chooses an advocate from their family to stand with them during the wedding ceremony. These advocates are the ones who will help the couple throughout their marriage should any disagreements arise or counseling be needed.

The cost of a church wedding, large village reception, building a suitable home and paying for all the required clothes, goats, household goods, as well as money to the family is often overwhelming to young couples. As a result many young people choose to run off together and start a family without any of the checks and balances that are built into a traditional marriage. These families often dissolve into polygamous relationships, and/or multiple affairs with very broken hearts and homes. I've counseled more women on the topic of polygamous marriages than all other topics combined during my ministry in Malawi.

When you question people about whether or not they are married, be sure to ask gently and be sensitive to their response. If the answers seem reluctant and your friend begins to close up, back off. You may have touched a very painful subject.

Ndasangalala kukuonani!

Ndah-sah-ngah-lah-lah koo-koo-oh-nah-nee

I'm happy to see you!

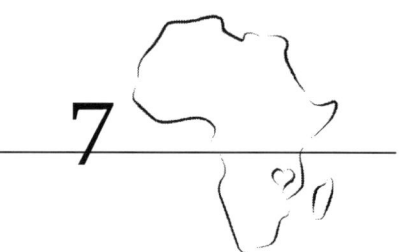

Practice

We are really starting to add on the syllables now. Chichewa has a lot of vowels and some words can get really long! Practice saying this one out loud to yourself several times before you try to say it to someone else. Then use it as your greeting today, *"Ndasangalala kukuonani.* I'm so happy to see you today!"

Go Deeper

Let's take a deeper look at this Chichewa for a minute. The verb *-sangalala* means to be happy. *Nda-* is the first person prefix for the immediate past tense. You have seen this in an earlier lesson with *Ndadzuka bwino* (I woke up great), *Ndaswera bwino* (I've had a great day so far) and *Ndayenda bwino* (I've traveled well). You can use this prefix with any verb to make the immediate past tense.

The verb *kuona* means to see. In order to say "to see you," we need to add the infixes for the polite object pronoun you. In Chichewa the polite object pronoun you has two parts: *ku—ni*. The *ku* comes before the verb root and the *ni* is added as a suffix at the end of the word. In this case, we would add to the verb *kuona* the infix *ku* and the suffix *ni*: *kukuonani*.

You've seen this before in the phrase: *Ndimakukondani*. I love you.

Let's look at two more verbs: *kupatsa* (to give) and *kuthandiza* (to help).

Kukupatsani means to give you. I want to give you a book. *Ndikufuna kukupatsani buku.*

Kukuthandizani means to help you. I want to help you. *Ndikufuna kukuthandizani.*

Pepani

Pay-pah-nee

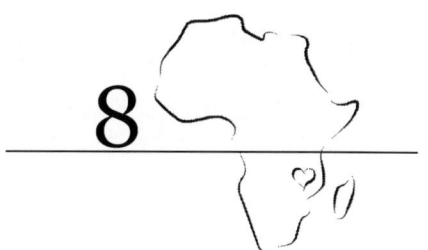

I'm sorry. Don't be upset.

Practice

Hopefully you will have to work to find some reasons to use this word today, unless you have a toddler nearby! Look for opportunities to comfort someone by saying, "*Pepani*. I'm sorry you are hurting."

Go Deeper

The verb *kupepa* means to cease to be angry or upset, to accept an apology, or to take a deep breath and cool off. We are using it in here in a command form. When you say to someone *Pepani*, you are encouraging them to calm down, please accept your apology or condolences, and to relax.

Pepani is in the polite form. You can say it very gently. It is not a harsh command, but rather a comforting encouragement.

You can use *pepani* when you are comforting a child who is crying or upset. You can use *pepani* at a funeral to comfort the grieving family. *Pepani* is also useful when you mess up and make a mistake. Keep it handy and be ready to apologize often. It is not easy to cross cultures, so always be ready to say *pepani* even if you think you're right.

Ask before you judge: another huge challenge for crossing cultures is our tendency to judge all things by our own worldview. We naturally assume the whole world thinks like we do and traveling to a foreign culture can open our eyes to the incredible diversity and beauty of differing worldviews, if we allow it to. Always ask about something you see, hear, or experience before you make a judgement of right or wrong. Most of the time, it's just different!

Amayi/Abambo

Ah-my-ee/ah-bah-mbō

Mother/Father or Mrs./Mr.

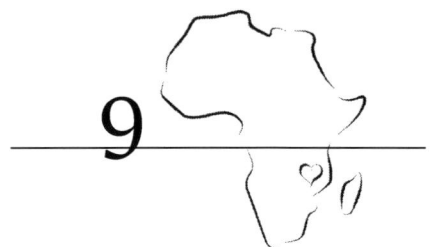

Practice

Try addressing your friends today as *Amayi* <u>insert name</u> or *Abambo* <u>insert name.</u> Try to use each word at least 20 times. For example: *Amayi* Melissa or *Abambo* John.

Go Deeper

Amayi and *Abambo* may become some of your favorite Chichewa words. It is just SO polite! You can call any woman *Amayi* and it is respectful and well received. *Abambo* works in the same way for men. The A- at the beginning of these two words are an extra politeness that can be put on the front of anyone's name to make it even more respectful. Banda is a very common surname in Malawi. When you address a man named Charles Banda as *Abambo* ABanda, you've shown great respect.

Respect is a highly valued character trait among Malawians. It is taught from infanthood. There are several things you may see that are ways of showing respect. Here is a short list of some respectful acts.

> Receiving something with both hands.
>
> Kneeling before someone to greet them.
>
> Kneeling before someone to speak with them, for example, a wife will kneel before her husband or a villager before a chief.

You can show respect by using polite titles when addressing someone for example: *Amayi* Banda or *Abambo* Charles. You can receive respect graciously when someone kneels before you to greet you. You can kneel to greet or speak with a chief or person in authority.

Abusa

Ah-boo-sah

Pastor

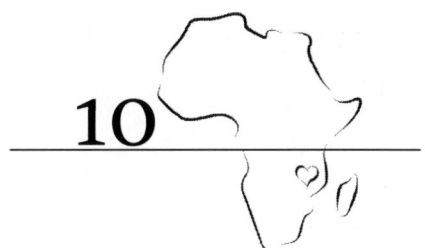

10

Practice

Try calling your pastor today and use your new vocabulary word, *Abusa*! It's a good time to talk with him about your trip to Malawi and to practice your Chichewa!

Go Deeper

I love discovery stories and one of my favorites is the story of how the very first Chichewa Bible translators figured out this word *Abusa*. In the late 1800s, Europeans were just beginning to filter into some of the deeper, inner parts of Africa. A missionary had been working for several months on translating the Bible from English to Chichewa but was failing to translate the word "pastor." He tried asking in many different ways, but nothing came up as a satisfactory word for this special position. Then one day, he was working on translating Psalm 23 and a group of goats was ushered past his house being herded by a shepherd. Quickly he rushed out to find his language helpers and discovered the word *mbusa*. In the polite form with the A- prefix, which we learned previously, the word *Abusa*, came to represent a shepherd of people, a pastor.

Pastors hold a very important position in Malawian culture. They are highly respected and are often looked to for help and guidance. In our Western culture, we expect to take care of our Pastor, to pay him a good salary, and make sure he has a home. In Malawian culture, people will often look to their pastor for assistance with food, clothing, home, etc. This can often cause strain in our cross-cultural understanding as pastors will then come to a missionary for assistance. The missionary thinks, "Go to your congregation for help." But the pastor knows his congregation is looking to him for help. You can look for ways to encourage and pray for pastors as they carry a heavy load caring for their flock.

Mwana/ana

Mwah-nah/Ah-nah

Child/children

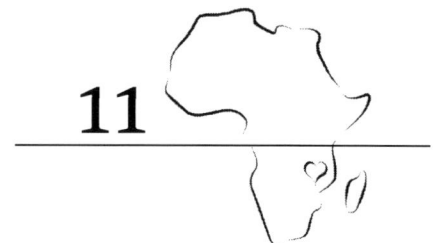

Practice

Time to teach some Chichewa! Find as many kids as you can today and teach them the word for children. If you don't see a lot of kids in your normal circles, try calling a family member with kids or volunteering for a local kids club. They'll love the extra hands and you can teach them about Malawi and the Chichewa words you've been learning.

Go Deeper

Ana! Ana! Children are everywhere in Malawi. One reason is that 46% of the population of Malawi is under age 14. The average family has at least 5 children, many have more than 8 or 9. Children in Malawi are always outside. The adage that it takes a village is certainly true here as the children roam through out the countryside on their way to school, following the most interesting thing on the path and chasing after a good soccer game!

No matter where you go, you will find children. They are normally very friendly and will delight in following you along your way and helping you carry your backpack. Just a head's up, someone, somewhere along the way taught Malawian children to say in English, "Give me money." This is probably the most annoying thing I've found in Malawian culture. My responses vary depending on my mood between a simple, "No!" to "Give me money" (holding my hand out). Occasionally I will lecture children on the evils of being a beggar and encourage them to stay in school and pursue a good career. Always keep your response polite, you are the visitor, but NEVER give money to a child. NEVER. Never give away water bottles, or candy, or anything you have with you unless you have a LOT and you have a controlled situation with a Malawian person of authority (a pastor or a teacher) to monitor the kids' response. You will be overwhelmed with "give me" the instant you start to give something away. **If you want to give, always give through your host to avoid causing more harm than good.**

Tiyeni

Tee-yeh-nee

Let's go!

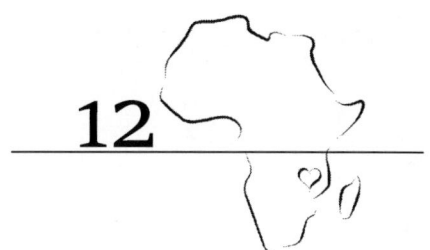

Practice

Tiyeni is just plain fun! Use it to stir up some fun today! *Tiyeni*; let's go grab a cup of coffee together! *Tiyeni*; let's have lunch today! *Tiyeni*; let's sit down for a nice long chat. Use *tiyeni* today to catch up with some friends and tell them about your trip to Malawi.

Go Deeper

Tiyeni! Every day we're getting closer to taking off for Malawi. Let's take some time today to learn more about this beautiful country.

A great place to start is with a Google search for Malawi images. You'll see pictures of Lake Malawi, grass-roofed huts, gardens, and kids in school uniforms. If you don't already know, take a few minutes to email your host about where you will be staying.

Next, do a little Google search for the place you'll be staying in Malawi. Read a few articles or blog posts about the people, agriculture, or culture of the area where you are headed.

Next, take a few minutes to read the CIA World Factbook about Malawi. You can type it into your search engine just like that.

Imagine how different life is now than it was for the first missionaries who ventured across the world to enter the African continent. Many of them packed their supplies in a coffin assuming they were going to die. They knew nothing about the people or the places they were going. They gave up everything to go share their love for Jesus Christ. I do not know your motivation for this trip, but I do know you are going to a country where the people have amazing, warm, kind hearts and where they live with joy in spite of extreme poverty. What sacrifice can you make; what can you give up as a part of your journey to Africa?

Sekerelani

Say-kay-lay-lah-nee

Laugh!

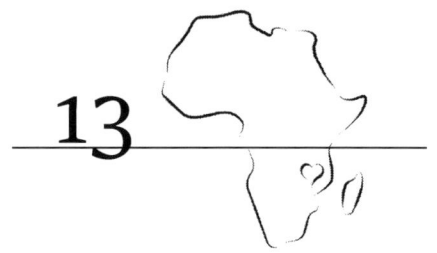

13

Practice

Get your camera out and practice saying, "*Sekerelani!*" See how many funny looks you can capture today as you tell you friends to "*Sekerelani*! Post the best ones to social media and share again about your upcoming trip to Malawi and how you're learning Chichewa!

Go Deeper

Kusekelera means to laugh or to laugh at something. It's not too hard to get a laugh from Malawians. Their country is called the "Warm Heart of Africa" for a reason! I've lived and worked in several African countries, but Malawians have the warmest hearts; their joy and laughter bubbles easily to the surface. I always admire the resilience of joy in the face of extreme poverty that I find in Malawi.

While laughter comes easily for Malawians, smiling for the camera does not. As soon as the camera comes into view one of two things happens: 1. stiff frowny faces or 2. goofy in your face poses. Don't get frustrated; just keep clicking! Thank God we live in the digital age and can delete the thousands of useless pictures it takes to get the prize. It is definitely worth your time to capture those beautiful smiles and precious faces so you can relive your Africa days over and over again once you return home.

You can try these other words for getting a better picture:

>Mwetulirani: Smile

>Musatulitse lilime: Don't stick out your tongue.

>Khalani pafupi: Get closer together.

>Sangalalani: Be happy.

>Suntani pang'ono: Move over a little.

Dzina lanu ndani?

Dzee-nah lah-noo ndah-nee

What is your name?

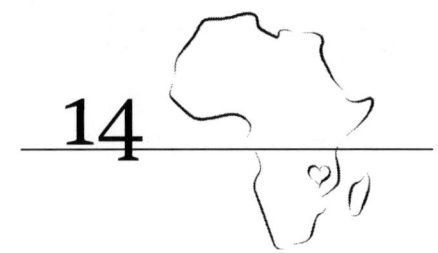

14

Practice

You may get some funny looks today as you ask your friends, "Dzina lanu ndani?" Go ahead and practice anyway! The bigger challenge when you get to Malawi will be to understand when the person answers! Shake off your fear and your embarrassment. You can't let little things bother you like people laughing—you've got a language to learn!

Go Deeper

Let's break down the question first of all: *dzina* = name; *lanu* = your, *ndani* = who. This is in the polite form so you can use this question to ask anyone, adult or child. Be careful when you are in Malawi to double check any phrases you learn from children with an adult language helper. As an expat, you should never use the impolite form in Chichewa, especially with an adult.

How do names work in Malawi? At birth, parents choose someone to name their baby. The parents have the right to veto the name, but this rarely happens. A person's name is comprised of their first name and their father's first name. For example, my first name is Karen. My father's first name is Robert. So my name would be Karen Robert in Malawi culture. Sometimes in marriage the woman takes her husband's first name. My married name would then be Karen Leonard. Often when a child is under the care of an uncle or a grandfather, he or she will be registered at school with that person's name. Names can get confusing!

In Malawian culture, it is often impolite to use an adult's first name. Note: This is changing in the 17 years I've worked in Malawi; however, it is always better to err on the side of politeness, especially with elderly people. When you are introduced to someone, use the title *Amayi* or *Abambo* in front of the name you were given to show your respect.

Ndikuchokera...

Ndee-koo-chō-keh-lah

I am from...

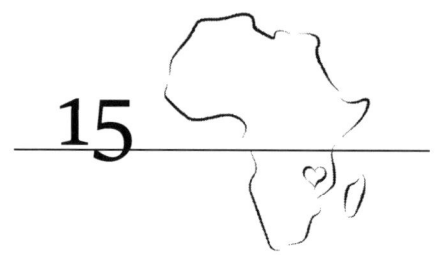

15

Practice

You know that game where you say, "My name is Karen and I'm from Kalamazoo, I'm going to Kansas, and I'm taking a kangaroo!" I want you to play a modified version of the game like this: I'm from ____ and I have a ____. Find these things in the English/Chichewa Google translator, and write the Chichewa word in the blank: dog _____, car _____, cow _____, ox cart _____, house _____, book _____, spoon _____, plate _____.

Now come up with a place that starts with the same letter. I'll help you with the first one: *Ndikuchokera* Georgia; *ndili ndi galu*. (I'm from Georgia; I have a dog.)
Ndikuchokera _____ *ndili ndi* _____.

Go Deeper

I grew up in 22 different houses in 4 states. As a result, I never developed very strong community ties to one place, so when I got to Africa and began to see how closely Malawians stay connected to their home village and family, it was a new experience for me.

In Malawi, a person's home village is always where they are from. It doesn't matter where they actually live now. This fascinates me! I almost feel lost somehow because there isn't a place where all my family comes from, where my grandparents and uncles remain, that I always go back to. A person's home village in Malawi is HOME, in Chichewa, *KWATHU*.

The Chewa culture is maternal, so often a person's home village is the village his mother comes from. Many times the family is raised in the mother's village. When a couple gets married the man must build a house in the woman's village. Children belong to the maternal family. In the event of the death of a mother, the children will be given to the maternal grandparents, aunts and uncles. In the death of a father, if the family has been living in the father's village, the mother and children will often be asked to return home to the mother's village.

Muli ndi zaka zingati?

Moo-lee ndee zah-kah zee-ngah-tee

How old are you?

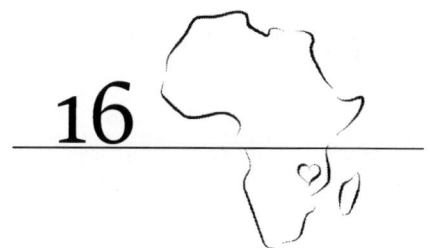

Practice

Try not to get yourself in trouble today as you practice asking, *"Muli ndi zaka zingati?* How old are you?" Remember you need to practice something at least 20 times before you know it, so ask 20 people today, *"Muli ndi zaka zingati?"*

Go Deeper

Literally, this question, *"Muli ndi zaka zingati?"* asks "You have years how many?" Let's break it down a little farther so we can use these same words in other questions.

Muli ndi means you have. You have a book. *Muli ndi buku.* You have a car. *Muli ndi galimoto.* You can easily turn it into a question by putting the word *Kodi* in front: *Kodi, muli ndi buku?* (Do you have a book?) *Kodi, muli ndi galimoto?* (Do you have a car?)

Zingati is the question word for how many. It gets a little trickier to use this word. Chichewa has 17 noun classes. Each noun class has prefixes that are used on the adjectives and adverbs to make them agree with the noun class. When we say *zaka zingati*, we are using the prefix for the zi class. You can ask *Muli ndi ana angati?* (How many children do you have?) You will notice we switched the prefix zi- for a- . It is difficult for you to learn all the noun classes, so just be aware they are there and use the words. Your friends will understand and will help you say it correctly. *Kodi, muli ndi _____?*

Birthdays in our Western Culture are very important. We teach our children their birthdate and how old they are from a very young age. This is not the case in most of Africa or in Malawi. Many adults know the year they were born, but they will have to figure out how many years it is when you ask them. Don't be surprised if your question is followed by a pause! Children will answer much more quickly, but don't be surprised if they make up their answer! They often have no clue how old they are, much less their date of birth.

Tipemphere!

Tee-pay-mphay-ley

Let's pray!

17

Practice

You'll want lots of people praying for you as your travel to Malawi, so get the ball rolling today by inviting people to pray with you. Even on our best days, it might be challenging to find 20 different people to pray with, so do your best and see what happens when you spend a day focused on prayer! *Tipemphere!*

Go Deeper

You will love the friends you make in Malawi. Their warm humor will give you plenty of opportunity to laugh together. I hope you also have plenty of chances to pray together. It will open your eyes to a whole new world!

One day while I was still learning Chichewa, I was leading a bible study at church. At the end of the lesson, I wanted us to pray together. I asked a few women to pray and then I asked one of the women I knew best to close our prayer time. At least that is what I thought I asked her to do. *Tipemphere*, I said and I prayed first. When I finished praying, this woman began to laugh right out loud for just a second then stopped. The next woman started to pray and when she finished this woman began to laugh again. I start freaking out a little on the inside. The third person prayed and as she finished the woman started laughing again, but this time the other women stopped her. WHAT ARE YOU DOING? They asked. I'm doing what Mayi Roller told me to do, I'm laughing in prayer! OH NO! To my credit, the only difference in the two words is a little t, *kutseka* (to close) and *kuseka* (to laugh). She went on to explain that she thought it was a strange thing to do, but since we had such a nice lesson together she thought it would be good to laugh. Okay. I could hardly get home fast enough. I don't even know how I stayed composed long enough to get out the door and run as fast as I could before collapsing in a puddle of hysteria.

I only have one story better than this; the time I said the food was made out of the Holy Spirit, but that's for another day. Don't let mistakes keep you from trying!

Ndidzakusowani

Ndee-dzah-koo-sō-wah-nee

I will miss you!

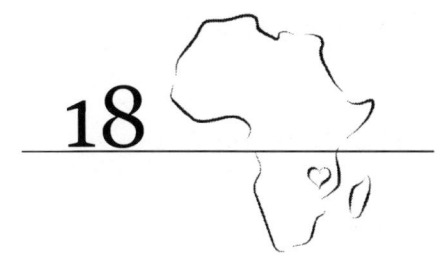

Practice

We are about ready to head for the airport, start letting your friends and family know that you'll miss them while you are gone. Tell 20 people today, "*Ndidzakusowani* while I'm in Malawi."

Go Deeper

Ndidzakusowani is a promise. It carries powerful meaning that a connection has been made between two people. In this lesson I want to warn you about the Promise Pitfall and give you a few clues how to avoid falling in yourself or pushing a Malawian friend into this trap.

Here is how the pitfall works. You are playing with the kids on the soccer field and one of the kids gets a stubbed toe. As you clean up his toe, you exclaim, "Oh, you should not be playing soccer without shoes! You need some shoes." Your declaration comes back to bite when the little guy reaches out his hand for a pair of shoes. You never meant to promise shoes, but you've fallen into the Promise Pitfall and an expectation has been set.

Here's another example: "I wish you could visit my home in America!" You have no intention of purchasing a ticket for the person to visit you; it's just something you say. Then the person goes to your host and announces that you invited him to visit America. When the ticket isn't forthcoming, your host is left in the hot seat with expectations that cannot be fulfilled.

Avoid the promise pitfall by keeping your conversation focused and practical. Ask questions but keep your exclamations to a minimum. Be careful and thoughtful when you speak. Talk about life in Malawi, the weather, family, crops, school, church and relationship with God.

Mwakhoza

Mwah-kō-zah

You did it!

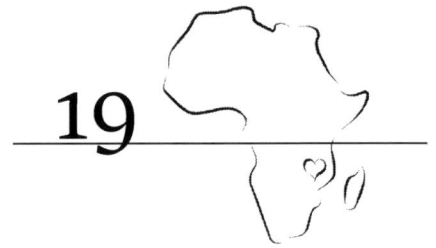

Practice

Let people know that they are doing a great job today by encouraging them with this little chant: *Mwakhoza! Mwakhoza!* Shoo-wah! It means, You did a great job! You did a great job! SURE! Make sure to say that last shoo-wah with a little flare!

Go Deeper

One of the qualities I admire most in Malawians is their perseverance. I've often said that if my children were dependent on me to carry water and grow all my own food, they would starve to death. In the onslaught of drought, poverty, starvation, and hard labor, Malawians are the most joyful, warm-hearted people I know.

I saw this Malawian strength on the face of a mother one day when I sat with her at the funeral for her daughter. Just a young school girl, she lost her life to some undefined disease. They carefully laid her body out for burial and then gathered around to mourn. Church members came from nearby villages and sang through the night and the next day to bring comfort and peace to the family. I was given a front row seat in the house right next to the little girl's body. Her mother was directly across from me. I watched her face as the grief wrecked her countenance. Her pain was real and so hard to see. Then as I watched, I saw her resilience as she joined singing the hymns. The battle of suffering and peace was fought out on her face that day. I will never forget how strong she was as the comforters came to help her up and lead her out of the house to the graveyard for the funeral.

Life in Malawi is hard. I say "*Mwakhoza! Mwakhoza!* SURE!" to my Malawian friends. I honor you and respect you for doing what I could never do. May God give you grace and meet all your needs.

Tsalani bwino!

Tsah-lah-nee bwee-nō

Stay well!

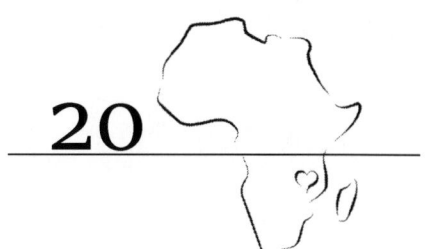

20

Practice

As you head out the door, be sure to tell everyone staying here at home, *Tsalani bwino*. They would say back to you, "*Yendani bwino,*" which means go well.

Go Deeper

Cross cultural good-byes can be rough. Many times we don't know if we'll have the opportunity to see each other again and while some of our Malawian friends have access to the Internet and social media, there just aren't any certainties in our farewells. For many of us, the whole Malawian experience has opened our eyes, wrecked our hearts, and expanded our world-view. It is not an easy thing to leave the friends and the place that have impacted us so deeply.

In the team journal* I use to prepare Circle of Hope teams for their Malawi experience, I've used this poem to help explain how I feel about good-byes:

> One last hug; wipe away another tear.
> One more good-bye; pick up my bag.
> One final wave; just get on the plane.
> My heart breaks;
> Broken pieces spread across the Atlantic.
> Africa seems surreal now.
> Like the dream of another time;
> Another me.
> I don't want to lose this Africa me.

Be sure to say your good-byes well! *Tsalani bwino! Yendani bwino!*

A Living Expression of Your Dangerous Love, Karen Roller & Dawn Cole, 2015. Available on Amazon.

Section Two

12 Conversations

The Pointing Game

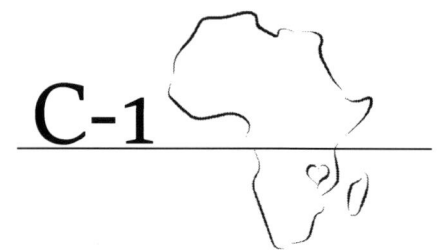

C-1

The simplest conversation we can have is mimicking words. Don't be afraid to start with this game. Simply walk around with your language partner and point to things. Don't worry about remembering every word, just try to hear what your friend is saying and mimic the sounds.

Point to objects around you and ask this question:

Ichi ndi chiyani? What is this?

Ichi mumati bwanji m'Chichewa? How do you say it in Chichewa?

After you've played this game for awhile, you might want to write down some of the more important things you've pointed to so you can practice them again later. The blank pages are provided for you to write words, draw pictures, or whatever is needed to aid your communication efforts.

If you can't find the item you are looking for, you may have to play a game of charades to figure it out!

Body Parts

Ziwalo za Thupi

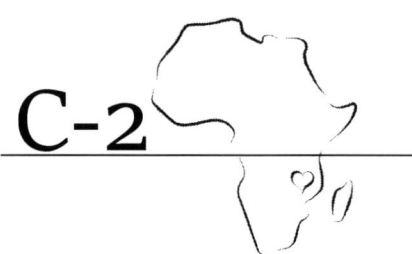

C-2

_____ hair
_____ 1 eye
_____ 2 eyes
_____ 1 ear
_____ 2 ears
_____ nose
_____ mouth
_____ tongue
_____ chin
_____ neck
_____ 1 shoulder
_____ 2 shoulders
_____ 1 arm
_____ 2 arms
_____ back
_____ stomach
_____ hips
_____ legs
_____ foot
_____ feet
_____ toes

Questions for use in a clinic or if someone is sick or hurt.

Are you okay? Are you hurt? (as in injured in an accident or while playing) **Muli bwino? Mwavulala?**

I'm sorry! Don't be upset! **Pepani. Pepani.**

Is your body hurting? (as in sick) **Mukumva kuwawa m'thupi?**

Where does it hurt? **Pakuwawa ndi pati?**

Show me where it hurts. **Mundilozele pamene pakuwawa.**

Have you been sick this week? **Munadwala sabata lino?**

What was your illness? **Chinavuta ndi chiyani?**

What is your illness? (right now) **Chakuvutani ndi chiyani?**

- Stomach = Mimba
- Diarrhea = Kutsegula
- Fever = Thupi likutentha
- Headache = Mutu
- Vomiting = Kusanza
- Coughing = Kutsokomola, Chifuwa
- A cold (also flu) = Chimfine
- Malaria = Malungo

Open your mouth! **Tsegulani pakamwa panu!** or **Yasamani!**

Stick out your tongue! **Tulutsani lirime!**

Let me look in your ears! **Ndiyang'ane nawo m'makutu.**

Turn around! **Tembenukani.**

Breathe deeply! **Pumani kwambiri!**

Do you have any wounds? **Muli ndi bala?**

Animals Around the Village

Nyama Zimene Zikupezeka ku Mudzi

C-3

Play a game where you act out animals and learn the names in Chichewa. Write them next to the animals or on the blank pages.

Learn the sounds an animal makes in Chichewa (don't be surprised if a rooster doesn't say cock-a-doodle-doo)!

Allow children to color the animals in your book.

Wild Animals
Nyama za ku Chire

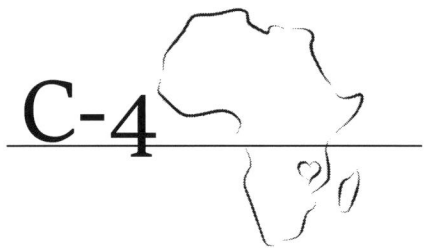

Things Around the Village
Zinthu Zimene Zikupezeka ku Mudzi

C-5

Kwathu = Home or home village

Mukuchokera kuti? Where are you from?

Ndikuchokera ____. I am from ____.

Mudzi wanu uli kuti? Where is your village?

Dziko Lapansi = the World

Dziko la Malawi = the country of Malawi

Playing Games
Masewelo

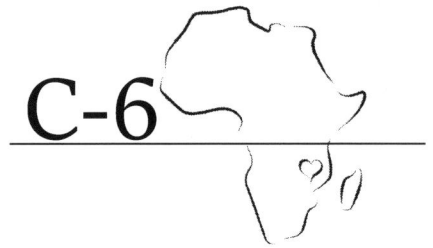

C-6

Kodi, mumakonda masewelo anji? What do you like to play?

Mundionetse masewero anu. Show me your game!

Mukhoza kundionetsa m'mene mumasewerela? Can you show me how to play your game?

Ndikufuna kuseweranso. I want to play again!

Tiyeni, tivine! Come on! Let's dance!

Tiyeni! Tisewere mpira! Come on! Let's play soccer!

Ndimakonda.... I love ...

    Kuvina = to dance

    Kuyimba nyimbo = to sing songs

    Kusewera mpira = to play soccer

    Kujambula zinthunzi = to draw

    Kusewera jingo = to jump rope

    Kusewera fulaya = a kind of dodge ball

    Kulumpha = to jump

Sindikumva. I don't understand.

Things at School

Zinthu Zimene Zikupezeka ku Sukulu

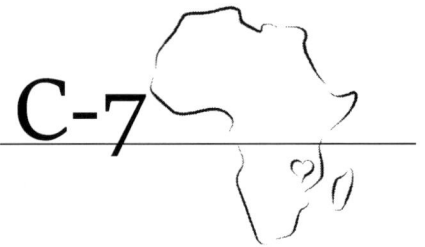

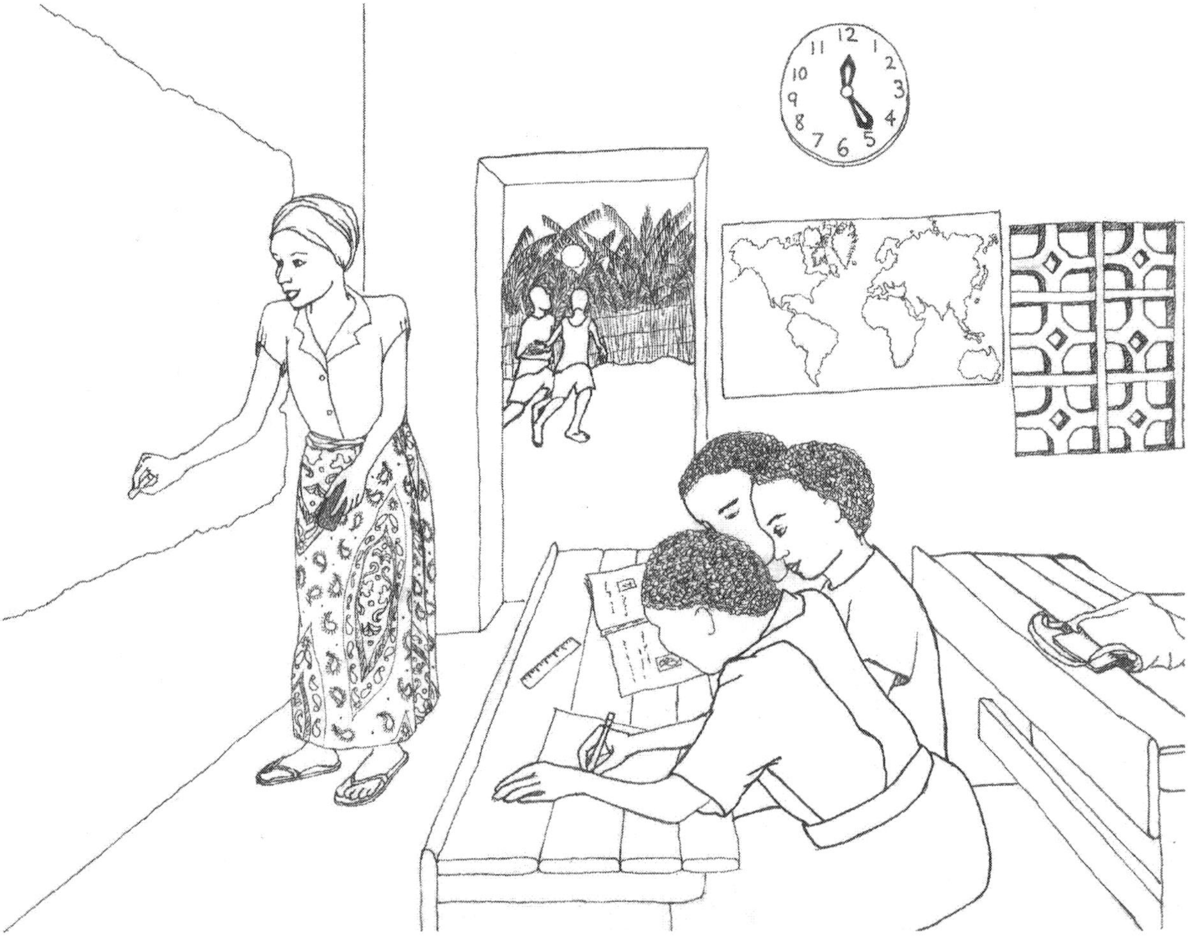

Talking about School

C-8

Mumayimba sukulu? Do you go to school?

Muli kalasi yanji? What primary grade are you in?

    In Malawi, Primary School is Standard 1 – 8. Secondary School is Form 1 – 4.

Mumayimba sukulu kuti? Where do you go to school?

Mumakonda phunziro lanji? What do you like to study in school?

    Some sample answers to this question:

    Masumu = Math

    Chizungu = English

    Chichewa = Reading

    Ulimi = Agriculture

    A-E-I-O-U (Pronounced AH-AY-EE-OH-OO) = Beginning Reading

    Kuyimba = Music

    Social = Social Studies

    Health or Life Skills

    Technology = Computers

    Biology

    Physical Science

By 8th grade all children are expected to take their National Exams in English. This does not mean that the children have very much conversational English, but as you see, most subjects have English titles and are often taught in English.

Do you speak Chichewa?

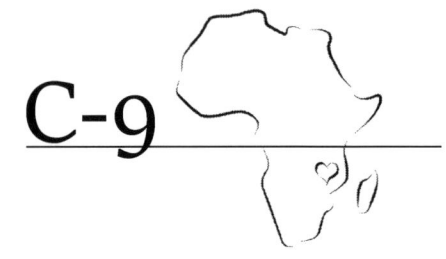

C-9

Mumalankhula Chichewa? Do you speak Chichewa?

    Ayi, sindikulankhula Chichewa. No, I don't speak Chichewa.

    Ndimalankhula pang'ono. I speak a little.

    Sindikumva I don't understand.

Mumalankhula Chingerezi? Do you speak English?

    Inde, ndimalankhula Chingerezi. Yes, I speak English.

Someone may alternatively say: *Mumalankhula Chizungu?* This also means do you speak English but it uses the slang word for English (*Chizungu*).

A few hints to remember when you get yourself in the middle of this conversation:

Zikomo = Thank you. You can never go wrong by thanking someone.

Clapping your hands together softly without a sound is a very polite when you are greeting someone or passing by on the path or road.

Smile! Smile! Smile!

Laugh at yourself often and don't get offended when people laugh at you!

Basi! = That's enough! Please, in this situation do not use this word with a harsh tone! Put on a smile, hold your hands up in front of you in surrender and say gently, "Basi!" One of my favorite stories with this word happened to a friend of mine. She was trying to get one of the children to stop misbehaving during chapel at our school. Very calmly and gently she was saying, "Basi! Stop it." He was not obeying. Another child looked her right in the eye and said "No, say it like a MOM!" She did and he immediately stopped what he was doing! In this case, don't say it like a Mom, say it like a friend!

My Family

Talking about Your Family

Iri ndi banja langa. This is my family.

M'banja langa, ndili ndi... In my family, I have...

    Ine, Ineyo = I, me

    Mwamuna wanga = my husband

    Mkazi wanga = my wife

    Ana anga = my children

    Mwana wamkazi = daughter; Ana akazi = daughters

    Mwana wamwamuna = son; Ana amuna = sons

    Mwana m'modzi = one child

    Ana awiri = two children; Ana atatu = three children; Ana four, five, six or however many you have. Once you get past three, just skip to English. You will find that Malawians will do the same! To your ears it may sound more like saying Folo, Fivie, Sexisie, Sevenie, Eightie, Ninie, Tenie.

    Mdzukulu/adzukulu = grandchild/grandchildren

    Example: *M'banja langa ndili ndi mwamuna wanga, ana akazi atatu, amuna awo, adzukulu atatu, ndiponso ineyo.* In my family, I have my husband, three daughters, their husbands, three grandchildren, and me.

Introducing Your Family

Awa ndi mwamuna wanga. This is my husband.

Dzina lake ndiye John. His name is John.

Uyu ndi mwana wanga. This is my daughter (or son).

Awa ndi ana anga. These are my children.

Dzina lake ndiye Sarah. Her name is Sarah.

There are no gender pronouns in Chichewa.

Asking about a Person's Family

Muli ndi banja? Do you have a family.

Muli ndi ana angati? How many children do you have?

Muli ndi achimwene? Do you have brothers? **Angati?** How many?

Muli ndi achemwali? Do you have sisters? **Angati?** How many?

Mumakhala ndi ndani ku nyumba? Who do you live with?

Ndimakhala ndi... I live with....

Mwana wanu ndi okongola. Your child is beautiful.

An Activity

Take extra paper with you and have children draw their families.

All about Work

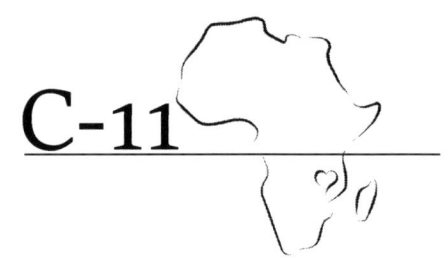

C-11

Mumagwira ntchito yanji? What is your work?

Ndimagwira ntchito ya... (Literally) I do the work of...

    Ophunzitsa = a teacher

    Odokotala = a doctor

    Ku chipatala = literally at the hospital

    Namwino = nurse

    Ulimi = farming

    Venda = business

    Oyendetsa galimoto = driver

    Ku banki = bank teller

    Za chuma = accounting

    Ubusa = pastor

    Ophika = chef

    Oyendetsa ndege = pilot

    Omanga nyumba = builder

Talking with Children about Occupations

Mukamaliza sukulu, mukufuna kugwira ntchito yanji? When you finish school, what work do you want to do?

A question for helping the children think about how to prepare for that future:

Kugwira ntchito ya _____, mukuyenera kuchita chiyani? What do you need to do in order to be a _____?

Talking about Jesus

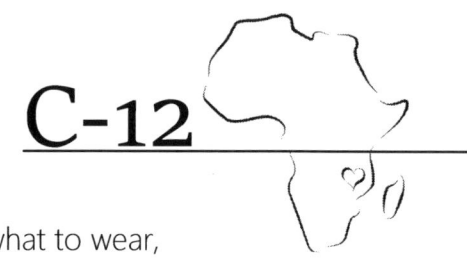

C-12

Every day we make choices. We make choices about what to wear, what to say, and what to do. **Tsiku liri lonse timasankha. Timasankha zimene tivale, tilankule ndiponso tichite.**

Some choices are good and some are not. Some choices lead us to sin. **Zisankho zina ndi zabwino, koma zina zimakhala zoipa. Zisankho zina zimatitsogolera ku matchimo.**

Sin separates us from God. **Matchimo amatisiyanitsa ndi Mulugu.**

When God created the world, He created man to have fellowship with Him. God loves us so very much. He wants to be with us all the time. He wants us to be able to choose to follow Him. **Pamene Mulungu adalenga dziko la pansi, adalenga Anthu kukhala naye m'chiyangano. Mulungu amatikonda ife kwambiri. Amafunitsitsa tikhale naye nthawi zonse. Amafuna kuti tili ndi mwayi kusankha kum'tsatira.**

So because of His great love, God sent His Son, Jesus Christ. Jesus died on the cross for our sin. He gave his blood to wash away our sin. Three days after his death, Jesus rose again from the dead! He conquered death and hell. Now, when we choose to receive Jesus as our Savior, we are no longer separated from God. **Tsono, chifukwa cha chikondi chake chachikulu, Mulungu adatumiza mwana wake, Yesu Kristu. Yesu adafa pamtanda chifukwa cha matchimo athu. Adapeleka mwazi wake kuchotsa matchimo athu. Popita masiku atatu pambuyo pa imfa yake, Yesu adaukanso kwa ukufa. Adagonjetsa imfa ndiponso Gahena. Tsopano, tikasankha kum'landira Yesu Khristu, Mpulumutsi wathu, sitikukhalanso patali ndi Mulungu.**

Now we can choose to receive Jesus. We can ask Jesus to forgive our sin and set us free from fear and evil. We can choose to receive the Holy Spirit to help us make good choices. **Tili ndi mwayi tsopano kusankha kulandira Yesu. Tili ndi mwayi kumufunsa kukululukira matchimo athu ndiponso kutimasula kwa zoipazo. Tili ndi mwayi kusankha kulandira Mzimu Woyera kutithandiza kupanga zisankho zabwino.**

We can receive the free gift of salvation, fellowship, and help for our every day needs—that's what we call grace! **Mwa Chisomo cha Mulungu, tikulandira mphatso wa ulele wa Chipulumutso, Chiyanjano ndiponso Chithandizo cha zosowa zathu tsiku liri lonse.**

Questions and Conversation Ideas

Have you received Jesus as your Savior? **Mwalandira Yesu Khristu kukhala Mpulumutsi wanu?**

Have you asked for the Holy Spirit to fill your heart and help you every day? **Mwalandira Mzimu Woyera kudzadza mtima wanu ndiponso kukuthandizani tsiku liri lonse?**

Do you want to pray to receive Jesus now? **Mukufuna kupemphera kulandira Yesu Khristu tsopano?**

Do you want to pray to be filled with the Holy Spirit now? **Mukufuna kupemphera kudzadzidwa ndi Mzimu Woyera tsopano?**

Let's pray! **Tipemphere.**

Do you like to read the bible? **Mumakonda kuwerenga Mawu a Mulungu?**

What is your favorite verse? **Mumakonda vesi yanji?**

I would like to read my favorite verse to you! **Ndikufuna ndikuwerengereni vesi imene ine ndimakonda.**

Do you know where we can find a Chichewa bible? **Tikhosa kupeza Buku Lopatulika kuti?**

Caution: Don't fall in the Promise Pitfall! If you ask the question, "Do you have a Chichewa bible?" the answer may be NO! with expectations that you will provide one.

Section Three

Glossary

A

Afternoon: masana

Agriculture: Ulimi (subject in school)

Airplane: ndege

Airport: bwalo la ndege

    I'm going to the airport. Ndikupita ku bwalo la ndege.

Also/too: -nso

    Me also/me too: inenso

    You also/you too: inunso

    We also/we too: ifenso

Always: nthawi zonse

America: Amerika

And: ndi

Angry (v) (to be angry): kukwiya

    Don't be angry with your friends. Musakwiye ndi azanu.

    What are you angry about? Mwakwiya ndi chiyani?

Animal/s: nyama (singular and plural)

Answer (v): kuyankha

    Try to answer the question. Yesani kuyanka funsoli.

Answer (n): yankho

    Kodi, yankho ndi chiyani? What is the answer?

    Mukudziwa yankholi? Do you know the answer?

    Mukhosa kuganiza yankholi? Can you guess the answer?

Ant/s: nyerere (singular and plural)

Apple/s: apozi (singular and plural)Arm/s: dzanja (singular); manja (plural)

Ashes: phulusa

Ask (v): kufunsa

    Ask your question. Funsani funso lanu.

    You've asked a good question. Mwafunsa bwino.

Aunt: Azakhali

B

Baby/babies: mwana (singular); ana (plural)
>I want to see your baby. Ndikufuna kuona mwana wanu

Back (body part): msana (singular); misana (plural)
>Does your back hurt? Msana wanu ukuwawa?

Backpack/s: chikwama (singular); zikwama (plural)

Backwards: m'mbuyo
>Kankhani pa m'mbuyo. Push backwards.

Bag/s: jumbo (singular); majumbo (plural)
>I need a bag to carry my things. Ndikufuna jumbo kunyamula katundu wanga.

Ball/s: mpira (singular); mipira (plural)
>We want to play soccer! Tikufuna kusewera mpira!

Banana/s: nthochi (singular and plural)
>Do you like to eat bananas? Mumakonda kudya nthochi?

Basket/s: dengu (singular); madengu (plural)

Bath (v): kusamba
>Ndikukasamba. I am going to take a bath.

Bath towel: chopukutira; alternatively a Chichewa form of English: bafa tawelo

Beans: nyemba
>We eat beans at school. Timadya nyemba ku sukulu.

Beard: ndevu

Beat (v): kumenya
>Beat the drum. Menyani ng'oma.

>Don't hit your friends. Musamenye anzanu.

Beautiful: -kongola
>The mountains are beautiful. Mapiri ndi okongola.

>Your baby is beautiful. Mwana wanu ndi wogongola.

>Your smile is beautiful. Kumwetulira kwanu ndi kokongola.

>Your eyes are beautiful. Maso anu ndi okongola.

>Malawi is beautiful. Dziko la Malawi ndi lokongola.

Bed/s: bedi (singular); mabedi (plural)

Bee/s): njuchi (singular and plural)

Beef: nyama ya ng'ombe

    Do you eat beef? Mumadya nyama ya ng'ombe?

Big: -kulu

    Big dog: galu wamkulu

    Big tree: mtengo yaikulu

Biology: (subject in school)

Bird/s: mbalame

Black: -kuda (This word can also mean dirty.)

    Black bag (or a dirty bag): chikwama chakuda

    Black dog (or a dirty dog): galu wakuda

    Black shirt (or a dirty shirt): Malaya akuda

Blanket/s: bulangeti (singular); mabulangeti (plural)

Blood: magazi

Boat/s: boti (singular); maboti (plural)

Body/bodies: thupi (singular); matupi (plural)

Book/s: buku (singular); mabuku (plural)

Boy/s: mnyamata (singular); anyamata (plural)

Bread: buledi

    I need to buy two loaves of bread. Ndikufuna buledi mwiri.

Breakfast: chakudya cha m'mawa

    Did you eat breakfast? Mwadya chakudya cha m'mawa?

    What did you eat for breakfast? Mwadya chiyani m'mawa?

Bridge: mlatho, ulalo

Brother/s: Mchimwene (singular), Achimwene (polite, plural)

Bus/s: basi (singular); mabasi (plural)

Buy (v): kugula

    I want to buy a Fanta. Ndikufuna kugula Fanta.

    I want to buy you a Fanta. Ndikufuna kukugulirani Fanta.

C

Cabbage/s: kabichi (singular and plural)

Car/s: galimoto (singular); magalimoto (plural)

Carefully: bwinobwino; chenjerani

    Hold the camera carefully. Gwirani bwinobwino.

    Be careful! Chenjerani!

    Carrot/s: kaloti (singular); makaloti (plural)

    Carry (v): kunyamula

    May I carry *insert name of child*? Kodi, mundirole ndinyamule _____?

    May I carry the bath water? Kodi, mundirole ndinyamule madzi osamba?

Cat/s: mphaka (singular); amphaka (plural)

Catch (v): kugwira

    Catch the ball! Gwirani mpira!

Chair/s: mpando (singular); mipando (plural)

Chalk: choko

Chalkboard: bolodi

Chicken: nkhuku (singular and plural)

Chief/s: mfumu (singular); mafumu (plural); the respectful singular is amfumu

Child/children: mwana (singular); ana (plural)

    My children: Ana anga

    One child: Mwana m'modzi

    Two children: Ana awiri

    Three children: Ana atatu

Chin: chigama

Choir/s: kwaya (singular); makwaya (plural)

Church/es: tchalitchi (singular); matchalitchi (plural)

City/cities: tauni (singular); matauni (plural); also, mzinda (singular); mizinda (plural)

Clap (v): kuomba m'manja; literally to clap hands

    Clap hands. Tiombe m'manja.

Classroom: kalasi

    Go into your classroom now! Lowani m'kalasi tsopano!

Cold (adj): -zizira
	Cold water Madzi ozizira
	I need some cold water. Ndikufuna madzi ozizira.
Cold (n) (also flu): chimfine
	I don't feel well, I have a cold. Sindikupeza bwino, chifine chikundimenya.
Cold, to be (v): kuzizira
	I feel cold: Ndikumva kuzizira.
	It is cold today. Kukuzizira lero.
	Are you cold? Mukumva kuzizira?
Come (v): kubwera
	Come here! Bwerani kuno.
Computers: Technology (subject in school)
Cook: kuphika
Cooking pots: poto, chiwaya, mphika
Corn: chimanga
Corn crib: kokwe
Cough (n): chifuwa
	How long have you had that cough? Mwadwala chifuwa nthawi yayitali bwanji?
Cough (v): Kutsokomola
	This child is coughing badly. Mwana uyu akutsokomola kwambiri.
Count (v): kuwerengela
	Count the children. Werengelani ana.
	Count these things. Werengelani zinthuzi.
Cow/s (also, ox/oxen): ng'ombe (singular and plural)
Crawl (v): kukwawa
	Has he/she started crawling yet? Wayamba kukwawa?
Crocodile: ng'ona (singular and plural)
Cry (v): kulira
	Don't cry! Osalira!
	Don't be upset! Pepani!
Cup/s: kapu (singular); makapu (plural)
	Please bring me a cup. Thank you. Bweretsani kapu! Zikomo!

D

Dad: bambo, dadi

    My dad: abambo anga

Dance (v): kuvina

    I like to dance. Ndimakonda kuvina.

    Let's dance! Tiyeni, tivine!

Daughter/s: mwana wamkazi (literally, female child) (singular); Ana akazi (plural)

Dawn/daybreak: kwacha

    How did your day begin? Kwacha bwanji?

Day/s: tsiku (singular); masiku (plural)

Desk: desiki, polembera

Dirt/dust(n): fumbi

Dirty (adj): -kuda (see black)

Doctor/s: dokotala

    Do you need to see the doctor? Mukufuna kuonana ndi dokotala?

Dog/s: galu (singular); agalu (plural)

Door/s: chitseko (singular); zitseko (plural)

Down: pansi

    Sit down. Khalani pansi.

    Put it down. Ikani pansi.

Draw (v): kujambula

    Draw a picture. Jambulani chithunzi.

Drink (v): kumwa

    He/she/they are drinking water. Akumwa madzi.

Drive (v): kuyendetsa

    I want to drive the car. Ndikufuna kuyendetsa galimoto.

Driver/s (n): dalaiva (singular); madalaiva (plural)

Drum/s: ng'oma (singular and plural)

    The boys are playing the drums. Anyamata akumenya ng'oma.

Duck/s: bakha (singular); abakha (plural)

Dust/dirt(n): fumbi

E

Ear/s: khutu (singular); makuto (plural)

Eat (v): kudya

    Let's eat! The food is ready! Tidye! Chakudya chapsya!

Egg/s: dzira (singular); mazira (plural)

Elephant: njobvu

English (the language): Chingerezi; Chizungu (slang)

Eraser: chofufutira

Evening: Madzulo

Excuse me: Pepani

Eye/s: diso (singular); maso (plural)

F

Face/s (n): nkhope (singular and plural)

Family: banja (singular) mabanja (plural)

Farm/s (n): munda (singular); minda (plural)

Farmer/s mlimi (singular); alimi (plural)

Fast (adv): mwamsanga

    You ran quickly! Mwatamanga mwamsanga!

Father: abambo

    My father: abambo anga

Fever: thupi likuthentha (literally, the body is hot); malungo

Finger/s: chala (singular); zala (plural)

Fire: moto

Firewood: nkhuni

Fish (v): kuwedza nsomba

    Do you like to fish? Mumakonda kuwedza nsomba?

Fish (n): nsomba (singular and plural)

Flower: luwa (singular); maluwa (plural)

Flu (also cold): chimfine

Food: chakudya (singular); zakudya (plural)
Foot/feet: phazi (singular); mapazi (plural)
Football (soccer): mpira (singular); mipira (plural); also just means "ball"
Fork/s: foloko (singular); mafoloko (plural)
Friend/s: Mnzanga (singular); Anzanga (plural)
    Close friend, special friend: Mnzanga wa pa mtima (literally, friend of the heart)
Friend/s: Bwenzi (singular); abwenzi (plural); often means boyfriend/girlfriend
    My friend: Bwenzi langa
Frog/s: chule (singular); achule (plural)

G

Game/s: Masewelo
    Let's play a game! Tiyeni tisewere masewelo!
Garden/s: munda (singular); minda (plural)
Gentleman/gentlemen: bambo (singular); azibambo (plural)
Gift/s: mphatso (singular and plural)
Giraffe/s: kadyansonga
Glasses (for eyes): galasi (singular); magalasi (plural)
Go: kupita
    Let's go to the store! Tiyeni tipite ku sitolo.
Goat/s: mbuzi (singular and plural)
God: Mulungu
Good morning: Mwadzuka bwanji?
Goodbye: Zikomo, ndapita. (Literally, thanks, I'm going.)
    Go well. Pitani bwino. *or* Yendani bwino.
    Stay well. Tsalani bwino.
Grandfather/Grandmother: Agogo wamwamuna; Agogo Wamkazi
Green: -biriwira
    I would like a green skirt (wrap). Ndikufuna chitenje chobiriwira.
Guard/s (n): mlonda (singular); alonda (plural); When calling the guard, use the plural to show respect if you are calling the guard.

H

Hair: tsitsi

Hammer/s: hamala (singular); mahama (plural)

Hand/s: dzanja (singular); manja (plural)

Handsome: wowoneka bwino (good-looking); wokongola (beautiful)

Happy: kusangalala; kukondwa

    I am happy to see you! Ndasangalala kukuonani!

Hardworking: wolimbikira

Hat/s: chipewa (singular); zipewa (plural)

Head/s: mutu (singular); mitu (plural)

Health (Life Skills): Thanzi; also, a subject in school

Heart/s: mtima (singular); mitima (plural)

Heaven: kumwamba

Heavy: -lemera

    You are so heavy! (As if talking to one of the toddlers) Mwalemera!

Hello: moni

Help (v): kuthandiza

    Help me! Thandizeni!

Herd/s: msambi (singular); misambi (plural)

    Goat herd:

Hill/s: phiri (singular); mapiri (plural)

Hippo: mvuu; bokho

Hips: nchafu

Holy Spirit: Mzimu Woyera

Home: nyumba

Homework: homu weki

Hospital/s: chipatala (singular); zipatala (plural)

How many/much?: -ngati

    How many things? Zinthu zingati?

    How many people? Anthu angati?

    How much (money)?: Ndalama zingati?

House/s: nyumba
Hurry: Fulumirani
    Hurry up! Fulumirani!
Husband: mwamuna + possessive pronoun
    My husband: mwamuna wanga
    Your husband: mwamuna wanu

I

Iron (n): chosita
Iron (v): kusita
    I need to iron my dress. Ndikufuna kusita dilesi langa.

J

Jacket/s: jekete (singular); majekete (plural)
Jesus: Yesu
Job: ntchito (also means work)
Joy: chimwemwe
Jump (v): kulumpha; kudumpha
    Let's jump rope! Tisewere fulaya.
    I can't jump very high. Sindingathe kulumpha kwambiri.

K

Kindness: chifundo
    He is kind. Ndi wa chifundo.
    You are kind. Inu ndinu wa chifundo.
Kitchen: khitchini
Knee/s: bondo (singular); mawondo (plural)
Know (v): kudziwa
    I know. Ndikudziwa.
    I don't know. Sindikudziwa.

L

Lady/ies: mayi; mzimayi (singular); amayi (polite singular) azimayi (polite plural)

Lake: Nyanja (singular and plural)

    We're going to the lake on Saturday. Tizipita ku Nyanja Loweruka.

Lamb/sheep: nkhosa (singular and plural)

Land (n): dziko

Later: nthawi yina

    We will have to do it later. Tidzayenera kugwira ntchitoyi nthawi yina.

Laugh: Sekerelani

Laundry (n): zovala zokuda (literally: dirty clothes) zovala zimene zinachapidwa (literally: the clothes that were washed.

    Where do I put my dirty laundry? Ndiike zovala zokuda kuti?

    Where is the clean laundry? Zovala zimene zinachapidwa zili kuti?

Laundry (v): Kuchapa zovala (literally: to wash the clothes)

    I want to help do the laundry. Ndifufuna kuthandiza kuchapa zovala.

    Where can I wash my clothes? Ndikhosa kuchapa zovala zanga kuti?

Leg/s: mwendo (singular); miyendo (plural)

    My legs are hurting. Miyendo yanga ikuwawa.

Lemon/s: ndimu (singular); mandimu (plural)

Letter/s: kalata (singular); makalata (plural)

    Did you write letters to send to your friends? Mwalemba makalata kutumizira kwa anzanu?

    Letters of the alphabet: malembo

Life Skills (Health): Thanzi (subject in school)

Lion/s: mkango (singular); mikango (plural)

Lip/s: mlomo (singular); milomo (plural)

    My lips are swollen. Milomo yanga ikutupa.

Lizard/s: buluzi (singular); abuluzi (plural)

Love (v): kukonda

    I love you! Ndimakukondani

Love (n): chikondi

M

Malaria: malungo
>I am sick with malaria. Ndikudwala malungo.

Man/men: bambo, mwamuna (singular); azibambo, amuna (plural)

Math: Masumu

Me: Ine

Minibus/es: minibasi (singular); maminibasi (plural)

Miss (v) as in miss the mark or goal: kuphonya
>You missed the goal. Mwaphonya goli.

Miss (v) as in to be without something; also to be in need: kusowa
>I will miss you. Ndidzakusowani.
>
>I missed you. Ndinakusowani.
>
>I miss our bible study class. Ndimasowa maphuziro athu a Mawu a Mulungu.
>
>I do not have enough food to feed my family. Ndikusowa chakudya chokwanira kudyetsa banja langa.

Monkey/s: nyani (singular); anyani (plural)

Moon: mwezi (also means month)

Morning: m'mawa

Mosquito/es: udzudzu (singular and plural)

Mosquito net: mosikito neti

Mother: amayi
>My mother is deceased. Amayi anga adamwalira.

Mountain/s: phiri (singular); mapiri (plural)

Mouse/mice: mbewa (both singular and plural)

Mouth: kamwa; at the mouth: pakamwa
>Be quiet! (as in a classroom): Chala pakamwa! (put your finger in front of your mouth). Children will generally respond "Wa" and put their fingers to their mouths.

Mrs: Amayi

Music: nyimbo
>I like this music. Ndimakonda nyimbozi.
>
>Would you like to hear some of my music? Mukufuna kumva nyimbo zanga?

N

Name/s: dzina (singular); mayina (plural)

    What is your name? Dzina lanu ndani?

    My name is ____. Dzina langa ndine____.

    What is his/her name? Dzina lake ndiye?

    His/her name is ____. Dzina lake ndiye ____.

Neck: khosi

Need (v); also want, seek: kufuna.

    I want bath water. Ndikufuna madzi osamba.

Night: usiku

    Good night! Usiku wabwino!

No: Ayi; basi (literally that's enough); toto (absolutely no, very emphatic, often with shoulders shrugging for emphasis)

Nose: mphuno

Now: tsopano

    I need to go now. Ndikufuna kupita tsopano.

Number: namba

Numbers: Most counting is done in English; however the numbers one through five and the number 10 are often used in Chichewa.

    One: -modzi

    Two: -wiri

    Three: -tatu

    Four: -naye

    Five: -sanu

    Six: zisanu ndi chimodzi; sikizi

    Seven: zisanu ndi ziwiri; seveni

    Eight: zisanu ndi zitatu; eyiti

    Nine: zisanu ndi zinaye; nayini

    Ten: khumi; teni

Nurse/s: namwino

    Call the nurse to help me. Itanani namwino kuti andithandize.

O

Okay: chabwino

Old: -kalamba

    My grandfather is very old. Agogo wanga akukalamba kwambiri.

    This shirt is too old. Malaya ikukalambadi.

    *How old are you? Muli ndi zaka zingati? (Literally, How many years do you have?)

On: pa

    Put your books on the table. Ikani mabuku anu pa tebulo.

Onion/s: anyezi (singular and plural)

Orange (color): olenji

Orange/s (fruit): lalanje (singular); malalanje (plural)

Ox/oxen (also cow/cows): ng'ombe (singular and plural)

Ox-cart/s: ngolo (singular and plural)

P

Pants (trousers): mathalauza

Paper/s: pepala (singular); mapepala (plural)

Pastor: Abusa

Peas: nsawawa

Pen/s: cholembera (singular); zolembera (plural)

    I'm looking for a pen. Ndikufufusa cholembera.

    Do you have a pen? Muli ndi cholembera?

Pencil/s: pensulo (singular): mapensulo (plural)

Person/people: munthu (singular); anthu (plural)

Picture/s: chithunzi (singular); zithunzi (plural)

Pig/s: nkhumba (singular and plural)

Pink: pinki

Physical Science: a subject in school, generally referred to in English

Plane: ndege

Plant (n): chomera

Plant (v): kulima

Plate/s: mbale (singular and plural)

Play (v): kusewera

> Let's play! Tisewere masewero!
>
> Let's play soccer! Tisewere mphira!
>
> What do you want to play? Mukufuna kusewera chiyani?
>
> Please: chonde; In Chichewa, the polite form of asking implicitly assumes the word "please." If you add "chonde" to your sentence, you will offend your host as this word is only used when the person has already turned down your request. Now you are begging him to reconsider. As a visitor, always use the polite form of the words. Only polite forms are taught in this book.

Porridge: phala

Pot/s: poto (singular); mapoto (singular)

Potato/es: mbatatesi (singular and plural); also called Irish

> Sweet potato/es: mbatata (singular and plural)

Pray (v): kupemphera

> Let's pray. Tipemphere!
>
> I will pray for you. Ndidzakupempherani.
>
> Will you pray for me? Mundipemphere.

Prayer/s: pemphero (singular); mapemphero (plural)

Price: mtengo

> I don't know the price. Sindikudziwa mtengo.
>
> Please ask the price of this item. Funsani mtengo ya chinthuchi.
>
> *What is the price? Kodi, ichi ndichi ndalama zingati?

Pumpkin/s: dzungu (singular); maungu (plural)

R

Rabbit/s: kalulu (singular); akalulu (plural)

Radio/s: wailesi (singular); mawailesi (plural)

> I heard the news on the radio. Ndimamva nkhani pa wailesi.

Rain: mvula

> Will it rain today? Kodi, kuli mvula lero?

Rat: khoswe

Read (v): kuwerenga
    Let's read a book. Tiwerenge buku.
    Will you read a book to me? Kukhosa kuwerenga bukuli?
    Would you like me to read a book to you? Mukufuna kuti ndikukuweregani bukuli?
Reading: Chichewa (subject in school)
    Beginning Reading: A-E-I-O-U
Recess: buleki
Red: -fiira
    Red cup: kapu lofiira
    Red house: nyumba yofiira
Relish: ndiwo
Repeat (v): kubwereza
    Repeat it. Bwerezani
Rhino/s: chipembere (singular); zipembere (plural)
Rice: mpunga
River/s: mtsinje (singular); mitsinje (plural)
Road/s: msewu (singular); misewu (plural)
Rock/s: mwala (singular); miyala (plural)
Room/s: chipinda (singular); zipinda (plural)
    Classroom: kalasi
Rope/s: chingwe (singular); zingwe (plural)

S

Sad: wokhumudwa
    Are you sad? Mwakhumudwa?
    Why are you sad? Mwakhumudwa chifukwa chiyani?
Salt: mchere
    Pass the salt! Ndikufuna mchere.
Sand: mchenga
Say (v): kunena
    How do you say it in Chichewa? Mukuinena bwanji m'Chichewa?

School: sukulu (singular and plural)
Score a goal (v): kugoletsa
   You made a goal! Mwagoletsa!
   Score! Score! Goletsani! Goletsani!
See (v): Kuona; to see each other: kuonana
   I see a hippo! Ndikuona bokho!
   See you later! Tionana!
Sew (v): kusoka
   I need to sew my trousers. Ndikufuna kusoka mathalauza wanga.
Shade (as in shade from the sun): mthunzi
   Let's sit in the shade. Tikhale pa mthunzi.
Sheep/lamb: nkhosa (singular and plural)
Shirt/s: malaya (singular and plural); shati (singular); mashati (plural)
Shoes: nsapato (singular and plural)
Shoulder/s: phewa (singular); mapewa (plural)
Sick (to be) (v): kudwala
   He/she is sick. Akudwala.
   I am sick. Ndikudwala.
Sing (v): kuyimba
   Let's sing. Tiyembe nyimbo.
   Do you like to sing? Mumakonda kuyimba nyimbo?
Sister/s: Mchimwali (singular); azichemwali (plural)
Sit down: Khalani pansi.
Skirt/s: siketi (singular); masiketi (plural)
Sleep: kugona
   Sleep well. Gonani bwino.
Slowly: pang'ono pang'ono
Smile (n): kumwetulira
   You have a beautiful smile! Kumwetulira kwanu kuli kokongola.
Smile (v): kumwetulira
   Smile! Mwetulirani!

Smoke (n): utsi

Snack (n): chakudya

Snake: njoka (singular and plural)

Snot: mamina

Social Studies: Social (subject in school)

Sock/s: sokosi (singular); masokosi (plural)

Son: mwana wamwamuna (literally, male child) (singular); Ana amwamuna (plural)

Song: nyimbo (singular and plural)

Soon: posachedwa

Sore/s (also wound/s, contusion/s): chilonda (singular); zilonda (plural); bala (singular); mabala (plural)

Sorry: pepani

Speak: kulankhula

    Do you speak English? Kodi, mumalankhula Chizungu?

Spider: kangaude

Spoon/s: supuni (singular); masupuni (plural)

Stand (v): kuima

    Stand up. Imililani.

Star/s: nyenyezi (singular and plural)

    The stars are beautiful in Malawi. Nyenyezi zili zokongola ku Malawi.

Stay well: Tsalani bwino!

Stick (n): ndodo

Stir (v): kutakasa

    May I help you stir the nsima? Ndifuna kuthandiza kutakasa phala.

Stomach: mimba

Stop crying: Pepani; Osalira.

Stream/s: mtsinje (singular); mitsinje (plural)

String/s: chingwe (singular); zingwe (plural)

Strong, strength: -mphamvu

    You are strong! (As if talking to a toddler) Muli ndi mphamvu!

    I am not strong. Ndilibe mphamvu.

Study (v): kuwerenga (also means to read)
    Study hard! Werengani kwambiri.
Sugar: shuga
Suit/s: suti (singular); masuti (plural)
Sun: dzuwa
Sweet potato/es: mbatata

T

Table/s: tebula (singular); matebulo (plural)
Tail/s: mchira (singular); michira (plural)
Tea: tiyi
Teacher: mphunzitsi (singular); aphunzitsi (plural and respectful)
Thanks: zikomo
That: icho (if you are pointing to something)
Thirst: ludzu
This: ichi
    What is this? Ichi ndichi chiyani?
Tie (n): tayi
Time: nthawi
    It is time to go home. Nthawi yafika, ndikupita ku nyumba.
Tired: kutopa
    I am tired. Ndatopa.
    Are you tired? Mwatopa?
Today: lero
Toe/s: chala (singular); zala (plural)
Together: limodzi; pamodzi
Tomato/es: tomato (singular and plural); matimati
Tomorrow: mawa
    Let's continue this tomorrow. Tipitirize mawa.
Tongue/s: lilime (singular); malilime (plural)
Tonight: usiku uno

Too: -nso
>Me too: Inenso
>You too: inunso

Tooth/teeth: dzino (singular); mano (plural)
Town/s: tauni (singular); matauni (plural)
Tree/s: mtengo (singular); mitengo (plural)

U

Umbrella/s: ambulera (singular); maambulera (plural)
Uncle: amalume
Under: pansi pa
>Under the table: Pansi pa tebulo

Understand (v): kumvetsa
>I understand! Ndikumvetsa!
>I don't understand. Sindikumvetsa.

Us: ifeyo, ife
>Come with us! Bwerani nafe.

V

Vegetables: masamba
>We should eat vegetables every day. Tikuyenera kudya masamba tsiku liri lonse.

Village/s: mudzi (singular); midzi (plural)
>Where is your village? Mudzi wanu uli kuti?
>Are there many villages near here? Kuli midzi yambiri pafupi?

Visitor/s: mlendo (singular); alendo (plural and respectful)
>The visitors have arrived! Alendo afika!
>I am a visitor here, please help me learn Chichewa. Ine ndine mlendo, mundithandize kuphunzira Chichewa.

Vomit: masanzo

W

Walk (v) (also means to travel): kuyenda, kupelekeza: to escort or go with someone
> Walk with me! Tiyeni! Tiyende pamodzi.
> I'm going home now, will you walk with me? Ndikupita ku nyumba tsopano. Kodi mundipelekeze?
> I will walk with you. Ndikupelekezani.

Want (v): kufuna
> I want bath water. Ndikufuna madzi osamba.
> I don't want to go. Sindikufuna kupita.

Wash clothes (v): kuchapa
> May I help you wash clothes? Ndikhosa kukuthandizani kuchapa zovala?
> Show me how you wash clothes. Mundionetse monga mumachapa zovala.

Wash dishes (v): kutsuka
> May I help you wash dishes? Ndikhosa kukuthandizani kutsuka mbale?
> Show me how you wash dishes. Mundionetse monga mumatsuka mbale.

Wash /bathe (oneself) (v): kusamba
> Wash your hands. Sambani manja!
> Go take your bath. Kasambeni.

Water (n): madzi

What?: Chiyani?

When?: Liti? (literally means "what day?)
> What time? Nthawi yanji?

Where?: Kuti?

White person/people: mzungu (singular); azungu (plural)

White: -yera; also: holy; clean
> White shirt: malaya oyera
> Holy Spirit: Mzimu Woyera
> White flour: ufa woyera

Who?: Ndani?

Why?: Chifukwa chiyani?

Wife: akazi + possessive pronoun (mkazi/akazi on its own just means woman/women)
> My wife: mkazi wanga

Wind: mphepo
> It is windy. Kuli mphepo.

With: ndi

Without: popanda

Woman/women: mkazi (singular); akazi (plural); mzimayi (singular); azimayi (plural)

Wood (firewood): nkhuni

Wood (as a material): mtengo (also means tree); lumber: tabwa (singular), matabwa (plural)

Word/s: liu (singular) mawu (plural)

Work (v): kugwira ntchito

Work (n): ntchito

Work hard (v): kulimbikira

Worker/s: wantchito (singular); antchito (plural)

Write (v): kulemba
> Let's write your name. Lembani dzina lanu.
> I will write you a letter. Ndidzakulemberani kalata.
> Will you write me a letter? Mudzandilembera kalata?

Y

Yellow: chikasu

Yes: eya; ee(long A sound drawn out a little); inde
> Yes, I finished my work. Ee, ndamaliza ntchito yanga.

Yesterday: dzulo

You: inu, inuyo (plural, polite) The singular form of you (iwe) is very rude to use with adults. Please take caution when learning words and phrases from children, check what you learn from them with an adult to make sure you are using the polite form.

You did it!: Mwakhoza!

Z

Zebra: mbidzi (singular and plural)

Printed in Great Britain
by Amazon